# *the* AWAKENING

**A Journey To Master Your Thoughts & Emotions,
Overcome Stress & Anxiety and Find Love within Yourself.**

FRANK OSAYI

# Copyright Page

First Edition Published by Frank Osayi

Copyright © 2021 Frank Osayi

WOW Book Publishing™

ISBN: 9798737795801

# DEDICATION

I dedicate this book to the real you, the joyful one, the one that is already peaceful within.

I hope that the words and message herein inspire you to reveal that part of you to the world.

Love,

Frank Osayi

# TABLE OF CONTENTS

# ACKNOWLEDGEMENTS

I appreciate the divine energy and higher powers that played a significant role in attracting the flow of events that were so powerful and fascinating that led to the manifestation of this book.

I acknowledge some of the souls that are no longer here such as Jim Rohn and Wayne Dyer for having such a positive impact in my life.

I'm grateful for some of the great minds that continue to pour into my soul such as Tony Robbins, Les Brown, Eckart Tolle, Michael B. Beckwith, Bob Proctor and many others whom I've not named but who continue to tirelessly help make the world a better place for you and me.

I would also like to thank my family, friends and supporters of this book for their encouragement and help in the process of creating it.

I now get to acknowledge you, the reader, for being on this journey towards self-awareness and beyond.

Thank you for having interest and taking the time to read about my journey and how you can learn from it.

I am thrilled for you.

# FOREWORD

*Dear Reader,*

*The Awakening is the book you need to read and learn about in order to discover who you really are on a level deeper than you can ever imagine.*

*Through his experience, Frank has acquired some deep knowledge about thoughts, emotions and its correlation with your daily choices and behavioural patterns; and he imparts it to you in a way that will allow you to understand it easily.*

*This book will take you on a journey beyond self-awareness so you can not only know who you are, but also build a strong relationship with who you are. It doesn't matter where you are on your journey, as you read this book, you will receive a shift in energy and consciousness that will create a deeper intimate connection with yourself that cannot be explained with words.*

*Most people spend their lives in search of happiness external of themselves. This book recalibrates your life in a way that leads to an ultimate sense of self-worth, self-love, Joyfulness and Peace within yourself.*

*It may take more than one reading and many hours of introspection, but The Awakening is a must-read for anyone in search of greater understanding of themselves and of the truth.*

*You've made a great decision.*

- **Vishal Morjaria**
Award Winning Author, International Speaker and Publisher

# CHAPTER 1

## UNEXPECTED AWAKENING

I t was late at night, and I was laid down on the couch in my sitting room. I had turned off the lights and was listening to a particular teaching from *Eckhart Tolle* while thinking about what I was going to do the following day.

As I listened and brooded over my schedule for the next day, different thoughts started to swirl about in my mind with each one consistently seeking my full attention.

I thought about a technical problem at work that

I had been struggling with, and then about what I would have for lunch and dinner. I thought about the next day's commute to and from work and all that I would have to do in between. I also found myself daydreaming about how I would score more than twenty points and help my team win the game at our next basketball competition at the local sports centre.

My legs were stretched out and crossed at my ankles. The back of my head was resting gently on my right arm. My eyes roamed around the sitting room before finally settling on the white wall beside the curtains. The TV's light was just bright enough to illuminate the corner of the wall where I spotted a scuff I had not noticed before. It looked like a stain that had been there for quite some time because it was at a height not easily reachable.

*How did that mark get there? And why am I just seeing it?* I thought. *Could it be that the stain had always been there, but I never spotted it?* I pondered for a while before my thoughts switched to getting rid of it and when I would get a chance to do so.

I thought it would be best to remove the stain with a damp cloth before trying the heavy-duty wall cleaner if that didn't work. After figuring out how to get rid of the stain in my mind, I decided to do it the next day before heading out to my basketball game. Although my physical body was in my sitting room, my consciousness however, had travelled far away. I was totally consumed in thought. The thoughts in my mind kept alternating between the stain on the wall, the technical problem at work and winning the basketball game. And then for a split second while rolling in and out of these thoughts, I would pick up snippets of Eckhart's voice from the TV.

A few moments later, just as I rolled out of thought, I heard Eckart's calm voice say '*You are not your physical body. You are energy expressing itself in a body*'. It was as if the words were whispered in my ears.

The words hit me with such great profoundness. I knew I had heard it before, but not with such resounding clarity and depth. The meaning of the words began to expand in my mind as my eyes were fixated on the wall; except this time, I didn't see the stain as I was utterly consumed in my thoughts. There was a slight pause on Eckart's teaching and for a moment there was no sound from the TV.

Then suddenly, I experienced something that I can only now describe as a dramatic awakening. There was absolute silence in the room. All my thoughts disappeared. My mind was empty but clear at the same time. I was just there with a blank mind yet with this vast presence. I felt a sort of detachment from my physical body. I could not feel my feet even though I could see them. It was a feeling and an experience unlike any I have had before. In that moment of absolute silence, it was like time stood still while I floated in space. It was as if the world around me had stopped existing, at least, for that moment. I began to feel like I was enraptured to a place out of this world. I could not feel my body, and it felt like I was not there but present at the same time. It was like I was seeing through my eyes as a separate being and not with my eyes like I usually would. I felt aligned with my source.

I vividly recall musing, 'Wow, I am not my body'.

After a short while, I slowly scanned the room contemplating, 'Wow. There's no end to this presence.' I felt a strong connection with everything around me. It was one of those experiences that would freak anyone out, but there was no hint of fear in me or confusion around me. The calmness that enveloped me throughout the experience remains unexplainable. In fact, I felt a deep lightness and sense of peace.

I felt free.

I'm not sure how long it lasted, but I was deeply mesmerized by the experience that I did not want it to end. Unfortunately, the TV's sound suddenly returned, and so did my consciousness, and the experience ended abruptly.

Like an unexpected storm hitting the coast, I felt a little wave of thoughts crash into my mind. As the thoughts rushed back in, I immediately regained awareness of my body and my surrounding, I could feel the couch pressing against my skin as it held the weight of my body. I could feel the air fill my lungs with each breath, the mark on the wall seemed dull again and my feet tingled as it pressed against the arm of the couch. I was not happy that the experience ended. The tranquility it brought made me long for more of it. I wished it had lingered a little longer. I wanted to relive it, so I reached for the TV remote control and turned off the TV. I tried to recreate the experience. Now laying in darkness on the couch I tried to force myself back into that state, I focused on emptying my mind, but it only ended in frustration. The more I tried, the more my mind raced with random thoughts. I kept getting distracted by thoughts of work, family, friends, and even the mark on the wall, which was no longer visible in the dark.

Disappointed and somewhat annoyed with myself, I gave up trying. But I kept wondering, *What if the sound of the TV didn't come back on? How long would I have remained in that state? Would I ever be able to get back into that state?*

The couch soon became uncomfortable as I had no answers to these questions. As a result, I went from laying on the couch; to sitting on the couch as I pondered on the questions that filled my mind like a new obsession. It was now crystal clear to me that my sense of self did not end with my physical body, but that I was something beyond my body. With profound clarity, I now understood the saying, '*You are not your physical body, You are energy expressing itself in a body*'. It was no longer just an intellectual understanding, but rather an experiential one. The experience triggered a paradigm shift within me that shook my very being. I knew my life would change. I had changed.

I could never be the same again.

# CHAPTER 2

## REUNITE WITH SELF

If you were asked, 'Who are you?' and you had to answer without using your names or nicknames, what would your response be?

Who would you say you are without identifying with your current and past generation of families? Who would you say you are without stating your age, gender, marital status, accomplishments, ethnicity, place or country of birth, current or previous addresses, professional and educational background?

Who would you say you are without talking about your likes, dislikes, hobbies, passions, and desires?

Who would you say you are if you had to omit all the aspects of life you have been conditioned to identify yourself by?

Have you ever thought about this question before?

If you haven't, that's okay because now you are thinking about it. So, what would your answer be?

Let me guess, you are not sure, right?

Now, I would like you to take a pause for a moment and attempt to answer the question because this is a crucial aspect of self-identification.

That's right. I know you did not attempt to answer the question the first time.

## More than Labels

You are probably wondering why I would ask you to answer the question without the usual labels. Or you may be wondering, can a person define themselves without any of the above descriptions? Can a person be anything other than these descriptions?

Before we conclude on any answer, let me share some insights that could guide your thoughts on the questions.

Your name is just something given to you by your parents; it is only a bunch of letters that confer an identity. Your name may have a deep or powerful meaning in itself, but it is just a label used to recognize you. Remember that you were already a living being before your parents decided to give you a name with which you would subsequently be identified. You were in existence before receiving a name, address, academic qualifications, and all other achievements you have had in life. So, the question is an inquiry into who you are before these identifications.

Your name is relevant to you and can somewhat acknowledge you, but it doesn't make you who you are. You were *you* before your name was given; you will remain *you* if it is taken away, so I ask again, who is that *you* that was named?

Similarly, your age is just a counter to how long you have lived; it doesn't explain what you have done, felt, learnt, or developed during that time. This implies that your age is the number of years you have been in existence on earth, excluding the period of your formation in your mother's womb. So, it should not define you.

Your current or previous locations are not who you are; they just happen to be where you once lived or currently live. Often, it is not even where you want to be; it is barely a stopover in your life's journey. As for your educational background, oh, how we love to attach so much importance to it, ignoring the fact that all it tells us is what you know or what you do. None of the above is a true definition of who you are because all of them are determined, affected, or influenced by others. In addition, you cannot identify yourself with the total sum of all your experiences because they are just a series of events, situations and circumstances that have taken place in your life's journey that you may or may not have had any control in.

You see, everything listed above is just what you acquired and experienced during your lifetime. Think about a baby at birth. When it arrives in this world, it has no labels. It is safe to say that your name, age, or location are just labels attached to the fact or duration of your existence. This is why you cannot identify yourself by any labels.

I hope this is beginning to make some sense now.

But if you cannot identify yourself by any of these labels nor experiences, then who are you?

If you are expecting me to give you a direct answer and tell you who *you* are, don't, because I cannot do that. No one can define you as you; only you can discover the

~

true you. What I can do, however, is assist you on your journey to self-discovery.

## Who Am I?

When thinking about the question 'who am I?' you might come up with several answers, including something like 'I am my *body*'.

Speaking of the body, let's do a critical examination of what this idea implies.

Let's say you are thirty years old right now. How many bodies have you been in since you arrived here on earth? Note that this has nothing to do with reincarnation. From the moment of your birth to date, you have undergone several changes in different bodies. I mean, look at the way your body has evolved with each stage of your life. It is simply an analysis of your transformation via your body as a vessel.

Let me break it down. At birth, you were in a baby's body. Most of us never remember anything from this time in our life, and that is understandable. Memories of you in the body of a baby may have been captured by your parents, guardians, or caregivers through pictures or videos. Then you grew into a toddler's body.

I remember some moments from my time as a toddler. Most of us do, and if we don't, our parents make a point of occasionally reminding us with embarrassing photographs. You may have seen yourself dressed in baby clothes, eating, crawling, attempting to walk and so on.

You kept growing, and before you knew it, you were in a 10-year-old body, adapting to society. I am sure that finding your place in this world was arduous at that point. Yet, as we grow older, we wish to go back to those days. How ironic!

Unfortunately, we cannot turn back the hands of time. Instead, your growth progresses, and in the twinkling of an eye, you are in a 20-year-old body. I still recall how young and vibrant I felt in my 20-year-old body. I was athletic and could perform all sorts of acrobatic moves, none of which I would attempt in my 30s. My body is not as flexible or fit for gymnastics as it used to be.

The Greek philosopher, Heraclitus, was right when he said, 'Change is the only constant thing in life'. Now, you are in your 30-year-old body, which is quite different from the first few bodies you had. Soon, you will be in your 40s and then your 50s. With each passing year, you will occupy new versions of your body unique to that segment of your life. This analysis helps you understand

~

what I mean by saying that you possess several bodies throughout your life.

Your body keeps changing. The change happens on a cellular level, and there will come a time when not a single cell of your 10 or 20-year-old body will be left.

When you were 12 years old, didn't you look in the mirror and see a 12-year-old body? This applies to every year of your life. The image you see in the mirror is just a reflection of the body that houses you as your years of existence progress.

This brings us back to the question at the beginning of this discussion: who is that '*you*' who keeps occupying the new bodies throughout your life? You should pause here for a moment and really think about this question.

## You and Your Thoughts

Do you identify who you are by your thoughts and mind? I mean, do you focus on your acquisitions   or accomplishments, or do you reflect on yourself as a consciousness with thoughts? Take a few minutes to intentionally channel your thoughts towards this question to produce a logical and coherent response.

When you were younger, you had ideas about

who you were and who you wanted to become. Your experiences and exposure might have influenced your decision to be one thing or the other when you grow.

As you grew up, you also had experiences that shaped and influenced how you act, react, think, dream, and even the things you desire. You developed more thoughts and ideas about yourself and your world. Each person develops differently, and the memories of your experiences will affect your thoughts and ideas as you get older. With each stage of life, these thoughts and ideas are likely to change several times. You also develop desires which can lead you on different paths in life.

Also, you meet someone, travel somewhere, or acquire new information, and your thought patterns are altered again and this continues throughout your life's journey. In other words, your thoughts and mind are constantly changing as you experience life. And with every change, there is *you* who is constantly witnessing this change. I don't think there is anyone in existence whose thoughts, ideas, or desires have not been altered at one point or the other in life. "Your thought patterns as a child are quite different compared to your 20s or 30s and beyond" hence, a substantial disparity between childhood and adulthood.

~

When I was six years old, my thought patterns revolved simply around food, sleep, school and play. In my twenties, my thinking patterns revolved mainly around relationships, college, travel and work. Can you relate?

So, who is the one that observes this constant change in thoughts and mind? Who is the person thinking all those thoughts? Who are you as a being with all these changes? This is something to ponder.

## Are You Your Emotions?

You may say you are your emotions, but you experience different emotions in your life, and sometimes within a day. Some of them come up when a thought comes to mind. Sometimes, emotions surface when something happens around you. And sometimes, you do not experience any emotions at all; you are simply emotionless. This implies that events and circumstances trigger your emotions. So, who is this 'you' that is filled with and expresses emotions?

To explore this more deeply, let us imagine that you leave your child in the sitting room for a few minutes. By the time you return, the child has made a mess. You would be angry or frustrated, either of which is an acceptable reaction. But who feels the anger or frustration?

Now, let us imagine that in the same instant, your child says, for the very first time, 'I wov you', in the cutest way you have ever heard it from a child. Would you still feel anger towards the child? Most likely, this innocent remark would soften your heart because, as humans, we are easily overcome by wholesome expressions of love. But there is still the lingering question of who is now feeling the love. Wasn't it the same you who felt the frustration a moment ago? So, within a short time, you have felt various emotions: frustration, anger and love. Who is the one feeling these different emotions?

## You as Self

So, if you are not your body, mind or emotions, then who are you? Who is this you that inhabits your body? What if I told you that you are the one who is trying to find out who you are? This, dear reader, is you.

You are the one seeking. You are the observer. You are the consciousness. You are like the space in which everything appears and disappears. You are the constant that keeps observing the change in thoughts, emotions and body. You are formless, shapeless and unchanging. Many names have been used to describe or define this

~

*you*; names like; 'inner- man', 'spirit-being' and 'soul', to name a few, but many do not understand that the moment you define something, you automatically put limitations on it. You are limitless and should not be defined. Whatever you may call it is unimportant; the important thing is that you recognise this essence of self.

Hopefully, you understand the concept of self as it relates to you without the identities given to you by others.

I believe we have now arrived at the identification of self. We can now continue this journey to unfold more of the 'you' that you didn't know about.

# CHAPTER 3

## RETREAT OR FACE THE

**L**et's say you are at an event that has lasted for some hours, and there is a networking session towards the end. Attendees are allowed to mingle, network, exchange contacts, or perhaps, fix a date to connect later, as the case may be. Imagine that you had spotted some persons earlier during the event, and you admired their mannerisms, eloquence, knowledge, wisdom, skill sets, accomplishments or whatever else it was about them that caught your attention.

What would you do when the opportunity to connect with them comes? Would you try to start a conversation with any of them? Would you move to make

friends or try to exchange contacts with them?

If your answer is 'yes', that is good. But why would you want to do any of that?

Let me guess: it's because you want to keep in touch, learn more about them, and maybe establish a relationship that will benefit you, right?

I want you to cast your mind back to any of such moments when you took a liking to someone you had met and wanted to connect or keep in touch with. You must have figured that you would have to approach them, introduce yourself, and start a stimulating conversation, right?

In other words, you knew that to build a successful relationship with them, you would have to spend some quality time with them because you understand that it takes time and effort to build a good relationship.

If that is how you would go about getting acquainted with someone else, why should it be any different when it comes to yourself?

Why don't you invest the same time and energy into getting to know yourself?

You have to learn to spend more time with yourself and launch into moments of deep self-reflection that will reveal your true self to you. Sadly, many people are too busy for this, and that's the reason they keep losing out on knowing who they are.

Are you one of such people?

Do you spend time with others but rarely with yourself?

Do you know other people more than you know yourself?

Do you spend more time getting to know others while you continue to live unaware of your true self?

It is one thing to know your true self but it is another to stay in tune with that self and work towards getting to know it intimately. You see, if you are ever going to stay in tune with anything, including yourself, you must connect and build a relationship with it. The way you try to develop a relationship with a person you admire or wish to befriend is the same way you should strive to do it with yourself. You will have to pay more attention to yourself and make out more time to be alone, not idle, but always *self-searching*.

How good are you at being alone?

Do you struggle to make out the time to be with yourself, or is this something you are already familiar with? Maybe you are an introvert who loves to be alone, but do you really spend time to hook up with yourself?

You may think you already spend enough time with yourself, considering the time you spend in the shower or restroom, playing video games, or lying on your bed and listening to music. You might also think the hours you spend watching movies or TV shows in your room late at night is equivalent to spending time with yourself. However, I urge you to reflect on those moments and consider what had your attention.

## Give Yourself Attention

Often, what we mean by spending time with ourselves is merely distracting ourselves. The bulk of our concentration is on one activity or the other, while we largely ignore our true selves.

How many times do you take your phone with you to the restroom and fiddle with it for minutes or hours? How many times do you go on social media when you hear the notification beep on your phone while watching movies, doing laundry, or lying down to rest? And by watching movies or TV shows, are you spending time with yourself or is that just another way to distract you from *you*?

If you are honest, you will agree that you are hardly ever present with your true self, even in your moments alone, because you always give in to the urge to engage in an activity. The mind always wants to engage in thinking and so it will always influence you into an activity to keep it going.

You may find yourself spending most of your time on one or more social media platforms daily because you do not want to miss out on your followership and the euphoria of being an online personality. If this is you, you are addicted to the distractions of life, which is unhealthy for your mental health, connection and relationship with your true self.

Are you terrified of being alone because you do not want to face your true self? You see, you won't make time to be tranquil if you are scared of interacting with or facing yourself. Activities—like drinking, playing video games, snacking, watching movies and using your cell phone are simply flights and escapes from intimacy with who you truly are.

Are you afraid of what emotions will surface if you are alone doing nothing? Or are you scared of facing the bitter truth that lies deep within you?

## Processing Your Negative Emotions

Most people have a lot of emotional pain and self-hatred buried deep within them, and they have never allowed themselves to process these feelings. Most times, the feelings you have been resisting for months or years will start to come up when you dare to have a moment alone with your true self. So, to avoid this, they need to structure their lives to always be busy doing things.

In life, you will go through adversities and face challenges that will cause you to feel certain negative emotions such as anxiety, grief, shame or loneliness.

You might be facing some of those emotions right now.

Rather than drown them out with constant activity, take time to process them. Unfortunately, you may claim to not have the time to do this right? And so you bury them because you feel it is the best way to deal with it. You escape those emotions for weeks, months, and even years. While you think they have dissipated on their own, they just keep piling up within. When you eventually decide to slow down or spend some time alone, they will start popping up one or more at a time, which could be very scary for most people. However, the fear of feeling these emotions has caused many people to keep suppressing them.

Processing these emotions could take weeks, months, or even years, depending on how often you are willing to self-isolate and deal with them. Any conscious attempt to suppress them will indeed alter your state of well-being, and they will keep coming. You will find yourself making decisions that may not align with who you are and what you want in life. But subjecting yourself to feeling these emotions enables you to remove the façade and face the reality that comes to you. The more you peel the layers off, the more you align with your true nature and stay in tune with yourself.

Besides, how do you know your true passion and desires if you have all these negative emotions clogged up within you? Imagine the considerable threat it will become to your focus and how that will sap your energy!

What if your life is designed to run on a different path from where you are now, but you are stuck in your present state because of this façade? What if you have lived your whole life, not knowing that your desires are not in line with your purpose?

Sometimes, you need to retreat from the world and divorce yourself from your daily routines that do not give you that inner connection or room for the growth of your inner self. This is an exercise I once adopted and continue to practice, and the benefits I saw prompted me to make it a part of my life. When I started self-isolating, lots of long-suppressed emotions began to surface. I could feel them bubbling within me—self-judgement, self-hatred and condemnation, the fear of not being loved, and—the most pressing one—the fear of death.

Processing these emotions was hard and uncomfortable, but I knew that the growth and connection with self, which I sorely needed, were only possible if I persisted. So, I kept at it, even though, at some point, it seemed as though I should give up and fall back into my usual routine.

To this day, the exercise is ongoing for me. I have integrated it as part of my daily activities, and the positive results keep encouraging me not to back down.

The more you process your emotions, the more you unpeel the façade that has covered and distracted you for a long time. And the more you peel away the façade, the more you reveal your true self.

When you start unveiling your true self in this way, you will begin to realise your actual reasons for doing certain things and why you have certain habits and quirks. For example, the exercise helped me discover

that snacking and eating late at night were habits I had unconsciously developed to escape dealing with my emotions.

When you match your emotions with your actions in this way, it becomes easy to spot those habits that do not serve you well, even though they appear harmless or normal. You will also notice a spike in your self-discipline, which will automatically increase your self-esteem and self-love.

You will be with yourself throughout your lifetime, so why not build intimacy with yourself and get to know it better? Your relationship with yourself is vital, and you should cherish it because it sets the tone for your relationship with the world and everything and everyone in it.

# CHAPTER 4

## THE ART OF DOING NOTHING

When you wake up in the morning, all of your five senses plug you into your external environment. They get activated and begin translating your world to you. Your eyes, which coordinate your vision, are calibrated to translate vibrations into sight. Your ears are equally designed to translate vibrations into sound, and the same goes for your other sensory organs.

All these sensory data are collected continuously and sent to the brain for processing. This can take a significant amount of brainpower. If the brain does not process these data, they cannot be interpreted, and your body function and perception will be rendered ineffective. Indeed, the function of the senses will become null and void. All these happen in split seconds, so fast that you don't even know they are happening.

## External Distractions

Based on research and observations, it has been established that most people's daily lives follow a particular pattern in this internet and social media era. You may be one of those people who grab their cell phones as soon as they wake up in the morning to check WhatsApp or text messages and even emails. Sometimes, you take a selfie and post it on Facebook; you *Tweet* something, check your Instagram page and start judging others unconsciously. Then you check the news and remember all the problems in the world.

Then you go to work and engage your mind by solving problems and dealing with colleagues and customers. Back home from work, you watch some television programmes and check all your social media accounts again. While eating dinner, you may also remain online to keep up with happenings before retiring to bed. Some people don't even sleep off when they get into bed; it has become customary to stay online while in bed. This goes on till late in the night or the wee hours of the morning. A good number of them drift off while still online, while others eventually have to force themselves to shut down for the night because of the following day's activities. They place their phones under their pillows before sleeping off, only to resume with it the next day, and the cycle continues again.

As a result of this habit, your brain and mind stay very active most of the day. Imagine doing this continuously for days, weeks, months, and years. If you pay enough attention, you will realize that most people are addicted to their phones. This is known as nomophobia. This is how many people live.

Not giving your brain and mind enough time to rest can lead to health problems down the line, especially if you are not getting enough sleep at night. And even if you are getting enough sleep, when you are asleep, you are unconscious and may not receive inspired thoughts and ideas. But when you decide to relax your mind, body, and brain while you are awake and conscious, you give room for transformative thoughts.

Besides, a decluttered mind is a fertile ground for inspiration and transformative ideas. You will also be able to examine your thoughts and process your emotions more clearly. This is why meditation is vital.

## All about Meditation

What does the word meditation mean to you? Do you think of it as a practice only for monks living in the Himalayan Mountains? Or you may have tried it before and labelled it a waste of time because you believe it did not work for you.

Meditation, in its most basic form, is simply the art of being conscious while doing nothing. It is about raising your awareness and surrendering to the present moment effortlessly. Your true nature wants to be conscious and present, but you usually get in the way by engaging yourself in excessive mind chatter or by exceedingly plugging your five senses into your external environment. This means that you can meditate anywhere, at work, at the park, or even in your car. Meditation is not limited to a specific location or time of the day. The key is to find a place where you can relax your body and quiet your mind for a few minutes, and this can be achieved by anyone, anywhere and anytime depending on your experience with it.

Let us go back to the moment when I experienced my unexpected awakening from the previous chapters.

What happened there? I was lying on the couch while staring at a stain on the wall, with Eckhart Tolle's voice playing in the background. So, my body was in a restful state, and the volume coming from the television was low and steady enough that my brain did not need to use much processing power to translate the sound. The lights in the room were turned off, except for the one coming from the television. With less light coming into my eyes, I had unintentionally reduced my mind and brain activity. Those little gaps of focused transition that lasted for a few seconds brought my awareness into the present moment. This was the sweet spot that allowed me to get into a meditative state, except I did not know this at the time.

The feeling I got from that experience was one that I had been seeking my entire life. It was a feeling of oneness and wholeness. Now, I know I experienced the spaciousness of what I am, the spaciousness of being. But I always thought I had to accomplish my heart desires or do something special with my life to get that feeling. I learnt that I could get that feeling while at home, doing nothing, just being quiet in my mind.

I also knew that I wanted to feel that way all the time and thus began my journey into meditation.

There are no prerequisites to meditation; however,

you should begin in your room with your doors closed if you are just starting out with it. This way, it will be easier for you to control your environment so you can simply 'be' and do nothing for some time without any distractions. If you are doing it for the first time in a public space, the chances are high that you would get interrupted and distracted, so your first trial should be indoors.

## Guided Meditation

If you are new to this, here is my meditation guide for you:

Find a comfortable chair in your room where you can sit up with your back straight. You can sit on the floor with your back against the wall or bed. I would avoid sitting on your bed, as this may cause you to fall asleep. Whatever position you settle for, ensure your back is comfortable and upright.

Ensure the lights are off; sometimes, the lighting in your environment can be a challenge or even a distraction.

You can put on a background meditation sound if you prefer, but if you do, set the volume as low as possible so that you almost have to listen for it. It must be as faint as possible to avoid it being a distraction. Whatever sound you decide to go with should have a steady tone to it throughout your meditation.

Ensure the temperature in the room is adjusted so you are neither too cold nor too hot. Any of these two can make you uncomfortable and nullify the process. Avoid eating or tasting anything during this time. There should be no variance in your sense of smell either.

The whole idea is to ensure your five senses are not being activated or overly stimulated at this time. You want them to be in a neutral state so as to reduce your brain and mind activity. Relax your body and you may close your eyes if you prefer. Remember, you don't have to focus on or do anything. You don't even have to breathe in a certain way. Let go of all expectations of yourself; you are not trying to achieve anything. Just sit there and *be*. Release every unnecessary energy that would cause you to focus your mind on anything in particular. Do not even try to relieve your mind of any worry or concern. Just forget about trying to do anything with your mind or body and just relax.

Many thoughts may begin to pop up in your mind. That's fine; just observe them. Don't try to fight them or try to stop thinking about them. Relax into the thoughts and think them through. After some time, you may be tense or worried that the thoughts just keep coming up in your mind; do not try to wrestle with it; just observe them. You may also remember the things you have to do later, which can lead to a lack of patience. Just pay attention to all that arises in you and recognise that they will soon pass. Understand that you are not your mind. Your mind does not have any power over you. You control the mind and not the other way round, and you may need to exert this control by bringing it under subjection and not allowing it take you out of meditation.

Remember, meditation is not about trying to clear the noise or thoughts in your mind, it's about recognizing that the noise or thoughts is not your identity. Interestingly, with this recognition, the mind eventually clears.

If you fall asleep in the process, be okay with it; do not pressure yourself. Falling asleep while meditating is simply your body telling you that it needs to rest, so don't let that stop you. You should realise at that moment that you may be overstressed and exhausted. That is a gentle reminder that you need to take more time to get enough rest. If you do not take care of your overworked body, it will break down one day. Ensure you get some rest after this attempt and try the meditation again the next day. If you fall asleep again the next day, this is also fine; just keep trying. Eventually, your body would have gotten enough rest that it requires to stay awake long enough to experience absolute silence in your mind.

Most people lack the patience to stick with it long enough to get to this state. They give up early, claiming to have had a bad or unproductive experience. Don't be like most people!

## Don't Give Up!

There is no such thing as bad meditation. Let's imagine you are trying to learn basketball for the first time, so you hire a personal coach to train you. Your dribble has no control at your first practice; your aim at the basket is entirely off, and you have no hand-to-eye coordination whatsoever. Now, imagine that after the first session, you turn to your coach and say, 'I am awful at this game; I don't think basketball is for me. Maybe I should just quit now'.

What do you think the coach will say to you? Of course, he will tell you that it was your first time, and if you keep at it for a while, you will develop the skills for the game. There is no such thing as bad training; each session ultimately compounds. Like many things in life, first, you will crawl at it, then walk before you can sprint. With meditation, it is no different.

A common idiom says, 'Practice makes perfect', meaning that the more you do something, the better you get at it. So, if you have not yet had a good meditation session, I would advise that you keep at it. Consistency is vital if you want to achieve anything in life. The process may not be achievable overnight, but consistency will help you get to a place of mental clarity and emotional stability.

If you find meditation difficult or a waste of time, that is perhaps because you are going about it the wrong way or you are trying too hard. You may think that you have to empty your mind or regulate your breathing or sit with your legs crossed in a certain way. You have probably assumed a specific method or pattern to meditation, which you have attempted to replicate with no success, and this has discouraged you from trying again. All forms of meditations are welcome. Another common idiom says "different strokes for different folks" implying variance in preferences from person to person. A form of mediation that works for someone, may not work for you. Be ok with this. Be willing to try other forms until you find the one that you are most comfortable with. But do not attach yourself to that exact practice, understand that it is just a practice to help you achieve clarity and awareness; and there are multiple ways to arrive at the same goal.

When you are new to meditation, it may take you up to an hour or two to get to absolute silence. You may struggle with it at first, but eventually, you will get rid of the mind chatter, or when the chatter comes, it will be in the background. And when you finally make it to silent mode, you will experience what it feels like to have clarity in your mind. It will feel like a complete 'lights out' in your brain. If you had music playing in the background at the lowest volume, the music would seem very loud when you enter this state of silence. This is because you are in a state of no thought, and so your hearing has been amplified. You will feel whole and at ease with life. All your problems and worries will seem to disappear in that instance. You wouldn't want the meditation to come to an end. This is what it feels like when you connect with your true nature. Until this happens to you, meditation will always feel like an abstract idea to you.

You may come out of your meditation with clarity on the next step to solve a particular problem or achieve some of your goals. The truth is that these steps are constantly flowing to you in the form of thoughts and ideas, but because there is so much *clutter* in your mind, they usually get lost in transit, or you brush them off because they do not resonate with you at the time. But with a clear mind, you will find yourself taking inspired action that does not feel like action at all because it is coming from a place of ease and joy. There is no resistance to it. This is one of the benefits of meditation.

Some other benefits of meditation are:

1. It helps you relax your mind.
2. It helps you control anxiety.
3. It reduces stress and puts your body in a relaxed mood.
4. It promotes emotional health.
5. It elongates your attention span.
6. It boosts self-awareness and gives room for inspiration and transformative thoughts.

Can you imagine living a life filled with fantastic benefits like these? What would you accomplish in your life? More importantly, how much fun will your journey become? You see, everything you need to live a joyful, happy, and peaceful life is already within you; all you have to do is connect to it more often.

Meditation is one of the surest ways to connect, and I believe this is what prayer should be about. When (or if) you pray, do you spend all your time talking and asking for things and never listening for the answers? Many of us are guilty of talking more and listening less; we fail to understand that listening is more essential than talking. When you speak, you only express yourself from what you know, but you create an opportunity to learn more and better understand when you listen.

Challenge yourself to do more listening than talking intentionally. Meditation gives you the chance to cut off all forms of distractions and opens your mind to more transformative thoughts and ideas. The next time you pray, I encourage you to talk for one minute if you have to and spend 30 minutes listening. You may be amazed by how loudly the universe speaks to you.

Spending time with yourself allows you to examine and evaluate your thoughts and explore your feelings. If you study the lives of remarkable people who make waves and do fantastic things, you will find that they mostly have one thing in common: they spend a significant amount of time with themselves. These people are at the apex of their businesses, careers, and fields because they recognise that the best thinking is done in tranquility.

Besides, you may not get your best insights in a noisy place or when you are surrounded by friends, but when you unite with your true self, you will receive transformative ideas in the absence of distractions and external interference—when your mind is crystal clear.

Silence and quietness are the new luxury in this

fast moving era that is filled with many distractions. Meditation is one of the best moves you can make to get your best thinking or insights, be more intentional in your daily activities, amplify your all-around productivity, and remain at the peak of your creativity. When you start taking it seriously, you will begin to hear the silent whispers of your greater self.

# CHAPTER 5

## YOUR INNER VOICE: A FRIEND OR FOE?

## The Mind Battle

Suppose you are part of the audience in a large professional setting or an event, and you think you know the answer to a question that has been asked. But just as you are about to speak, a voice halts you and says, 'What if your response is stupid? I'm sure you don't want to look stupid in front of everyone now, do you? It is better if you say nothing than give a foolish answer'.

Before you can silence this discouraging voice by confessing your strength, the same voice pops up to echo it by saying, 'That's right. You know there are dignitaries here, and you don't want to be seen as a fool'.

At this point, you are confused. You begin to entertain doubts about the answer you were once sure of. While you sit there thinking, you are encouraged by a voice of positivity.

'Just say it. If you are right, you will look smart in front of everyone; if not, you get to learn something new or the right answer. Also, this could be your moment to be in the limelight!'

With this mental pat on the back, you gather yourself back in one piece, and just as you are about to respond, the first voice returns, 'Hold on a second. You may want to re-think your answer because if you are wrong, you will be laughed at and ridiculed'.

For a few seconds, your mind jogs back and forth as you try to settle on a course of action. While this battle drags your concentration from the event, someone else rises and gives the same answer you were thinking of. There is a sudden calmness in your mind as the words echo in your head. Your curiosity is charged, and your eyes dilate as you listen with rapt attention to the reply from the person who asked the question.

You want to know if the answer is correct—to test your intelligence, validate your self-esteem, and challenge your resolve. You want to see if you just missed an excellent opportunity to advertise yourself as an intelligent person. Maybe that would have attracted more attention to you, and people of good repute would have desired to acquaint themselves with you. You would have benefitted so much from that simple, singular act of sharing what you know with people. The response comes in two simple words, 'That's correct!'

Suddenly, you feel a strange heat in your chest, and a chill runs down your spine as your temperature drops. A wave of applause breaks out for the bold one who disobeyed the same discouraging voice to speak up, clinching the moment.

The discouraging voices in your head suddenly become dumb and disappears while the cheerful voice throws you into guilt, saying, 'You see what I told you? You should have given your answer'. You can do nothing more, so you take the whip of guilt and recline into your chair. You exhale and reboot for another opportunity, which may never come again that day. But you have learned your lesson, and you know better what to do next time if such an opportunity comes your way.

Many people have had this experience once or more in their lifetime. I have, too.

## Another Scenario

Imagine you decide to go to the gym in the morning, so you set your alarm before bedtime. As soon as the alarm rings at 6:30 a.m., some funny conversations begin to pop up in your head as though two people are fighting for your attention. One of them wants you to go ahead with your plan for the day, while the other seeks to make you go against it. The conversation may go this way:

'It's 6:30 a.m., and you should be at the gym by 7 a.m. You should get up now'.

'No! You have not gotten enough rest. You should sleep for a few more minutes'.

However, you know so well that the 'few more minutes' could stretch into an hour, and you'd end up missing your gym appointment.

The voices keep fighting in your head.

'If you don't get up now, you might not make it to the gym by 7 a.m., and you know that!'

'That's true, no doubt, but you can get an extra 5 minutes of sleep and still make it in for 7 a.m. An extra 5 minutes will not harm'.

'Right, but what if I sleep past 7 a.m.?'

'You won't. It's just 5 minutes, something like a quick nap'.

'But what if I sleep beyond 7 a.m.?'

'Well, if you do, there is always tomorrow, right? Good thing, you're not answerable to anyone even if you decide not to go. It's just an exercise, and there's no big deal'.

At this point, you may find yourself thinking that having a good rest is not a bad idea. Then you tell yourself, 'That's true. I can always go tomorrow'.

'Yes, you can go tomorrow. Besides, tomorrow is Saturday, and Saturday evenings are better at the gym because it won't be crowded than what you'll see today'.

So, you go back to sleep, only to wake up at 8 a.m. and realise that you should have gone to the gym earlier because you already fixed other appointments for Saturday evening with people you cannot afford to disappoint. You then begin to regret your decision and blame yourself for not carrying out your initial plan.

Have you experienced something similar to this?

Does this internal dialogue happen whenever you are about to make decisions similar to those in these stories? Sadly, we often give in to the negative one and end up regretting it.

## My Experience

When I decided to start putting this book together, I had similar internal dialogues in my head. They were so loud that I almost got talked out of writing this book. The exchanges went something like this:

'What makes you think you are qualified to write a book? What life experience do you have to share? Remember you failed Literature in English in high school, so what writing skill do you have?'

Another voice replied, 'Yes, but I have a lot to share about my life and other experiences that people could benefit from'.

'People only read from people who have done or achieved something significant globally, like Steve

Jobs, Tony Elumelu, John Maxwell, Barack Obama, Bill Clinton, Ngozi Okonjo-Iweala, and Elon Musk'.

'But some people have written bestselling books before achieving any form of success in their respective spheres of relevance', the other voice countered.

'Yeah, but who cares about you and your boring personal stories? What do you have to share with the world that someone else has not already shared, and in a better way?'

'I guess you are right. I better wait until I have achieved something significant or become popular before writing a book'.

The negative voice in my head dominated me for a while and hindered me from starting this book. Whenever I decided to write, the negative voice would return and scatter my writing schedule, leaving me at the point of mere wishes. This went on for weeks and months until I came across an author who had published two books to help kids deal with bullying at school. She used her life experiences as the basis of her stories and had thousands of readers raving about her books worldwide. She was only fourteen years old.

I was both shocked and amazed at such a feat. *How*

*was it possible for her to have achieved that at such a young age?*

She did not wait to acquire a significant amount of success before writing from a bigger and more experienced perspective. She was proud to share what many people would consider 'a little experience' in her book. People already loved it, even adults who were far older and supposedly more experienced than her.

I concluded that this must mean that the voice in my head that convinced me not to write was not a friendly one. I was also convinced that the same voice must have been talking to the girl or had even told her worse things, but she overcame it through her resolve, which was why she started and finished writing a book.

You see, those voices in your head will never stop battling for your attention. They influence your daily choices positively or negatively. Your everyday decisions dictate your actions, and your actions—compounded over time—will eventually determine the result in every area of your life. So, if your inner voice plays a huge role in governing your results in life, how do you know which one to trust? Since both voices are coming from within you, how do you know a friend and a foe? To answer these questions, we have to examine the source of each voice and understand what influences them.

As you experience life, you begin to form a personal opinion about almost everything, consciously or unconsciously. These opinions are influenced by many factors, such as your family background, friends, experiences, information, and environment. If you grew up in the Middle East, you would almost always have a different personal opinion about your world than someone who grew up in Africa or the West. These personal opinions are what shape your attitude and thought patterns.

## Understanding Your Thought Patterns

Think of it like a thermostat that controls the heating system in the house. When you walk into your sitting room and it's freezing on a winter evening, you can either put up with the cold or set the thermostat to a favourable temperature so that you can go about your business more comfortably. As an example, if you set the thermostat to 30 degrees Celsius, the thermostat will regulate the room temperature for you. Whenever the thermostat detects that the temperature is below 30 degrees, it sends a signal to the gas burner to turn on the heater to keep the house warm.

While the heating process is on, the thermostat monitors the room temperature to ensure normalcy. The moment it detects that the room temperature is equal or above 30 degrees Celsius, it sends a signal to the heating system to stop. If you open your front door for a few minutes, the room's temperature will drop again, and because the thermostat is set to regulate room temperature at 30 degrees, it will signal the heater to start heating the room again. This cycle continues as long as the thermostat is on and programmed to regulate your room's temperature within a set degree.

The heater does not act on its own; directions from the thermostat control its actions. The thermostat, on the other hand, gives the prompt and commands a change or an action. It does not do the work of turning the gas burner on or off; it simply sends signals to the heater and the desired action is activated immediately.

The point in the illustration above is that the collection of your opinions about the world is like the thermostat. Your perception of things programs it. So, when you are faced with a challenging situation, signals are sent to your mind in the form of thoughts   to be processed based on this programming. This will lead to you experiencing these thoughts as inner voices speaking to you. These inner voices will attempt to take over your mind and lure you to take actions that suit the programmed settings.

The combination of these opinions is the controller; the thoughts and inner voices are the signals, and when you act based on these signals, you are like the heater that does what it is asked without question. So, to understand if you should accept or reject the voices in your head, you must first ask yourself: what temperature is your thermostat set to?

Rather than focus on the inner voices, you are better off paying attention to the opinion you have about each subject. Your current opinion could be clouded by shame, anger, disgust, irritation, judgement, fear, or other negative emotions that govern the subject.

When it became evident that my opinion about writing a book was clouded by judgement and fear, and my chances of going ahead were getting slimmer by the day, I had to take the bold step. I had to fight the negative voice and the fear it had introduced into my mind, including the fear of spending so much time to write a book that no one would want to read, and judgement from others about having the audacity to write a book when I have not yet achieved anything significant or record-breaking in my life.

In my experience, the only people that wrote books were those who were extremely intelligent and had good writing skills, or who had achieved something great and were celebrated for it. They were people with techniques and secrets that people would beg them to share.

This opinion was immediately laid to rest when I came across the 14-year-old author of two books. I started researching other authors and learned that anyone could write a book, regardless of their educational level, background, or financial success. The mere act of my continuous research significantly reshaped my opinion about writing. I came to believe that anyone could write a book if only we can shun the voices in our head, which keeps giving us a thousand and one reasons why we should not do it.

This internal shift helped me overcome the negative voice in my head and gave me the courage to write a book. Just like the thermostat, my programming changed, and I started receiving thoughts that convinced me that my experiences so far have qualified me to write a book on anything.

## Winning the Negative Voices

"My book does not have to take the whole world on a ride. I just have to write and share my experience and knowledge, and those who are ready for my book will benefit from it greatly. Everyone on the planet does not have to receive my book with equal feeling or perceive it the same way." This was what my new inner voice told me every day, simply because I had changed the setting of my thermostat on the subject of writing a book.

Let's go back to the example I shared earlier in this chapter about answering a question at an event. What happened there was simply the fear of judgement from speaking up in public, which was influenced by a negative inner voice telling you that the answer you had in mind was wrong.

Similarly, your resolve to keep your gym appointment was not strong enough; hence, the negative voice in your head, which was louder, succeeded in talking you out of it. Whatever your thermostat is set to on any given subject will become the most audible voice in your head. You may have experienced this type of inner dialogue in many ways and on different occasions in your life. Think of a time you were worried about something. You may have been so anxious that you lost your sleep.

All the voices and thoughts in your head may have told you that everything would soon go wrong. Out of all the possible outcomes, don't you find it interesting that your mind almost always chooses the worst-case scenarios for that event to play out? Again, the source of those thoughts stems from the collection of your opinions about various subjects combined.

You probably have desires or goals that you want to accomplish, but the voices in your head are keeping you from launching into action. Maybe you keep hearing the negative voice telling you that you can't make it, you're not fit or qualified, or things are going to crumble on you. Suppose you are fighting this battle at the moment. In that case, one of the effective ways to change the setting of your thermostat is to intentionally immerse yourself in situations or environments that interrupt and challenge those opinions you have built overtime for that particular subject.

If you persist in this exercise, you will eventually shift your opinions about it and change your programming. But you will first need to be open to this shift. And if you find that the inner negative voice is loud and gradually getting out of control, you may need to switch to meditation. As discussed in previous chapters, meditation will bring you back to a neutral state so you can have more clarity.

The more you meditate, the more you quiet your mind and connect to your inner self. When you tune in often, you will receive impulses that will help you differentiate between the friendly voices in your head and the ones that breed fear, shame or judgement.

This understanding will bring change to your mind and positively influence your attitude towards life. When those inner voices arise again, you will be able to observe, differentiate, and choose which of them to obey without having them control you or getting consumed by them. It will also help you to become conscious of those unconscious habits and thought patterns that are not serving you. You will no longer let any unwanted thought slip past your awareness and sink into your subconscious without you allowing it. The most important is that you will be able to identify the sources of the voices and decide to change the stories you tell yourself.

# CHAPTER 6

## IT'S TIME TO CLEAN THE FILTER

D o you feel good or bad most of the time? Or have you become so numb to your emotions that you can't even tell the variance of your feelings? Often, you hear people say that you have to take responsibility for your actions because they determine your results in life. But how often do you hear them say you have to take responsibility for your feelings? We have established in the previous chapters that your feelings precede your actions, which means your results are directly linked to your emotions. For that reason, don't you think it is high time you paid more attention to your emotions?

When someone pays you a compliment or gives a positive remark about you, it makes you feel good. On the other hand, if someone verbally abuses you or throws a negative remark at you, you may feel grief, anger, hurt, or all three emotions at once. In the same way, if you make some money or get a promotion at work, you feel joyful, but if you lose some money or get fired from work, you feel sad. In a nutshell, if something good happens in your life, you feel excited, but if it is something bad or negative, you feel frustrated, stressed, or sometimes disappointed. In other words, the emotions that you feel or express are influenced by things that happen to you externally. Don't you find it odd that an external experience can shift your inner world emotionally?

If you are like most people, multiple things could activate negative feelings within you on any given day. Let's say you are driving and someone suddenly cuts you off without a signal, or you find yourself stuck in traffic while you are running late for a meeting. Maybe you receive an email or notification from a particular person, and before you open it, you feel worried. It could be that someone challenges you in a debate or conversation, or you feel troubled about some future event. In a day, you can feel joy, frustration, happiness, excitement, anger, fear, hurt, irritation, jealousy, shame, despair, doubt, envy, disappointment, and even sadness. All these emotions are stirred up within you at different times, triggered by occurrences around you. Do you pay enough attention to your feelings to recognise that you go through an emotional rollercoaster within the course of a day?

You are probably seeing your life being explained as you assimilate these words.

## What Triggers Your Emotions?

If you are running through life constantly adjusting your emotions based on circumstances, the truth is that your life will be precarious and chaotic. You will end up taking actions that do not align with your true nature. These actions will eventually lead to unwanted results. Unwanted results will only make you feel even worse, and the cycle goes on.

I am sure that you have attributed how you feel inside to external occurrences for most of your life. I do not fault you for thinking this way because that is what it seems like. But what if I told you that these circumstances do not create your emotions? And that you are actually in charge of your emotions! You control how you respond to these circumstances and what feeling you express each time. It is your interpretation of these circumstances that cause you to feel the way you do. The power lies with you. It is entirely in your control. And if it is in your control, it means it can be changed. You can change how you respond and feel about occurrences in your life; after all, you own the body that houses and expresses these feelings. Recognising, this is the beginning of your journey to emotional mastery.

When an external event happens in your life, you perceive it with one or more of your five senses. What you perceive goes through a self-imposed natural filter, and based on your filter, you think positive or negative thoughts about that circumstance. Your thoughts automatically trigger a positive or negative emotion that causes you to react to the occurrence. This happens almost instantaneously, such that you are not aware or conscious that a thought preceded the emotion.

Notice that your filter interprets the event and assigned meaning to it, not the event or circumstance. For example, if you get a promotion at your job, the event goes through your filters. Your filter then associates the promotion with more money or recognition, and you start thinking about how you might be able to save more money to buy a house or how this will boost your career.

Your filter interprets it this way because you have seen people get recognition for their promotions or make more money and have better careers. These types of thoughts trigger a good feeling within you.

The peripheral assumption is that this positive emotional feeling stems directly from the event. Still, you created the emotion based on how you perceived and interpreted the event in the real sense.

If you get fired from your job, you equally perceive it through your senses. Your filters interpret this event as no more source of income, no recognition, and financial vulnerability. The thoughts that come up in your mind are thoughts of desperation, like how you won't be able to pay your bills in the coming months or how you may have to find cheaper accommodation or even become homeless. As a result, the emotions triggered within you could be worry, anxiety, fear, shame, stress, or even disappointment. You may have made plans and financial commitments, but now that you are out of a job with no other source of income, the reality is that your plans have become unrealizable at the moment.

It may seem like these negative emotions stem directly from the loss of your job, but your translation of the event is the reason for your negative emotion. It is the meaning you have attributed to losing your job that causes your suffering. If you think about it from a general perspective, the event is neither good nor bad. Your thinking makes it one or the other due to the meaning you have associated with the event. Remember that life is still unfolding around the world even after you have lost your job. In fact, many people worldwide may have lost their jobs too, but life keeps going on for them and everyone else. We cannot deny that many people have taken drastic measures due to their interpretation of such adverse circumstances. We hear stories of self-harm and even suicide due to these victims' reactions and succumbing to the overwhelming nature of these negative emotions.

## Who Controls Your Emotions?

There are also people out there who don't get sad or feel fear or worry when they lose their jobs. And it is not because they didn't love their job or they were not happy with it. It is simply because they have taken control of their filters consciously or unconsciously. They quickly begin to think about the next thing and how to get the next job. They don't waste any energy on stressing or fretting. Any energy or time you waste regretting or worrying about things you cannot change is gone forever and cannot be retrieved. These people are in control of their emotions, not the other way round.

You can do the same thing if you intentionally begin to pay more attention to yourself. When an event happens and you start feeling a negative emotion, let this be your guide: grab the thought from your mind and then reach for its opposite. If you were thinking, 'How will I pay my bills in the coming months?' you can replace it with, 'Well, I was able to find a job before, why won't I be able to find another job now?' Better still, you can change the narrative with a different perspective like, 'There are many job opportunities out there. Maybe this is my chance to find another job that I will love and enjoy even more'.

The idea is to start thinking general thoughts instead of focusing on a particular thought that will make you sad in the long run. An example of thinking general thoughts in the case of losing your job would be moving from "How will I pay my bills in the coming months?" to "I am not sure if I will find another job in time to pay my bills, but I will try my best to find one". This way you are not overly positive about the situation, but neutral about it. If you think more neutral thoughts about the situation, surely a momentum will build up where you will find it easier to think positive thoughts about the situation.

It is sometimes challenging to go from a negative momentum of thoughts to a positive one. Thinking in the general sense of things will bring you back to a neutral state, and from the neutral, you can slowly work your way to positive momentum. If you find it challenging to go general in this way because you have gone deep into a negative momentum of thoughts, you can ask yourself, *'How will I experience this moment if my mind did not get involved?'*

This is a question I always ask myself, when my mind focuses on the external event and extrapolates the worst case scenarios. This question does not really have an answer on a conceptual level, however, the mere act of stopping and asking myself this question allows me to become more present in the moment. You see, if my mind did not get involved in the moment, then there's nothing to think about, and all I am left with is awareness. I start noticing that I am maybe sitting or standing, I notice that I am breathing in and out, I look around the room or wherever I am at the time and pay attention to my surroundings in the present moment. Then suddenly, I will feel a weight lift off my shoulders in the moment.

If you can continuously become conscious of your filtered thoughts this way and start aligning your feelings with your thoughts, you are on your way to emotional mastery. You can clean out your filter by catching those thoughts and reversing them or letting go of the meaning you have assigned to them. The simple act of doing this is self-parenting, and it puts the control back in your hands. You will no longer be running through life, creating by default. You will become a conscious creator who has regained their power; you are now entirely in charge of your thoughts, emotions, and reactions.

## You Are in Charge

When you don't know about your filters, you will waste time trying to deal with the actual emotions or circumstances. Every emotion you feel is your indicator. They let you know what your current thought patterns are. The emotional triggers are not the enemy. Stop trying to fight it. Could you imagine if you had no emotion to guide you in this way? You would have thought patterns that make you take specific actions, and you would be unable to differentiate between your emotions. So be grateful for your emotions and see them as a gift. They allow you to evolve. This type of thinking is self-loving.

As I stated earlier, if you allow yourself to be controlled by happenings around you that trigger negative emotions, they will taint every form of happiness you should enjoy. Note that being in control of your emotions and thoughts is an intentional act. Do not allow yourself to sink into depression, sadness, anger, or any of the negative feelings usually associated with when events do not occur as you anticipated. Try as much as possible to view circumstances from a different perspective to not succumb to negative emotions and slide into depression.

For instance, the loss of a job can be viewed as an opportunity to try your hand at something different or acquire a skill you have always longed to get but never had time for. A rejected proposal can be a chance for you to expand your knowledge about that project and upgrade for future purposes. A critical and unbiased analysis of every occurrence that we usually refer to as negative will reveal many positive sides embedded with new opportunities.

You can realign your reaction to circumstances in your environment by first acknowledging that your well-being is a priority, irrespective of how your emotion translates the event. Now that you have been enlightened about how your emotions react, you can put them in check and take control of the way you respond to occurrences, whether they are anticipated or not.

It is undeniable that your thoughts would wander every day as you get involved in various activities. But for the sake of your peace of mind, you must do all that you can to detach yourself from your thoughts. The intention here is to gradually remove yourself from any negative thought that may eventually lead to negative emotion. Constant, conscious monitoring of your thoughts will weaken every form of negativity, and then you can slowly and steadily replace it with positive thoughts. This conscious effort has to be crowned with monitoring your focus to ensure that your mind does not stray from what you intend it to be on.

If you take your mind from negative thoughts and do not replace it with the proper focus, there is a tendency to slide back. To avoid this, you must consciously have an alternative focus for your attention. You have to intentionally guide your attention to focus only on what is necessary for your well-being and self-satisfaction.

The ability to train your thoughts, mind, and attention requires a lot of practice and consistency. I have explained how critical consistency and meditation are in previous chapters. Meditation is one of the practices that will aid your quest to keep your thoughts, mind, and focus under check. It will also help you to be in absolute control of your emotions. When you have total control of your emotions, you will not react negatively to external events like you used to.

One of the fundamental aspects of self-mastery is to develop emotional stability. It is a vital strength to have. It is the secret to a joyful life. If you find that you are constantly stressed, struggling, or worried about things in your life, this skill will help you remain calm but alert, relaxed but ready, smooth but sharp, humble but confident, patient but determined. You will be more resilient and know how to feel good even when the external environment is against you.

It is time to stop putting the responsibility for how you feel internally on external factors or other people. You know too much now to let that happen again. You now understand that most of the events that occur in your life are neither good nor bad. However, it is the meaning you assign to them that causes you to think a specific thought and feel a certain way. You are now in charge of your emotions.

CHAPTER 7

FEELING GOOD IS YOUR ONLY DESIRE

66

W hat are the things that trouble you regularly? I mean, those things that weigh you down and make you unhappy? Can you remember the incident that happened to you a few years, months or weeks ago, maybe days or hours ago? I mean, that thing that stressed you and made you feel like you were never going to come out of it. That time you felt like the world had come to an end for you, and giving up seemed like a better option.

Perhaps you got separated from your partner, failed an exam that truncated your ambition, or had a car accident. Whatever it was, it stole your joy at that moment and stirred some pain and unpleasant feelings within you, I believe you can recall it. Can you remember your thought process and your state of mind at the time?

You probably thought your life would never be the same again, and you didn't see any possibility of coming out of the situation unscathed. But today, you think back on those days and realise that you overcame every one of those problems, some of which seemed to disappear into thin air in the process of time by themselves.

Have you noticed that this cyclically happens to you?

Looking at your life in retrospect and how things are going presently, it seems like you are either coming out of a problem or currently facing a tough one. Then, when you encounter the next problem, you immerse yourself in the same thought and emotion patterns as though it's the first problem you have faced?

Why do you think this happens? Why do you always forget that you survived the problem that preceded the current one you are facing?

Now, you may probably be saying to yourself, 'Well, every problem comes with its unique challenges'.

This may be a fair point, but looking back to all of the problems you have survived in the past, as unique as they were, don't you think you could have still gone through them without feeling the pain, sadness, and despair that you allowed to overwhelm you? I'm willing to bet that you didn't solve any of the problems with your emotions, did you? So why do you always allow yourself to be triggered over and over again when you know that stirring your emotions at every challenge that comes your way does not contribute to the solution?

Perhaps, your argument is, 'Well, I am only human, and we are designed to feel all of our emotions.

As accurate as this is, however, you can build up your emotional strength, and we are supposed to do that as we pass through troubles. These challenges are supposed to make us stronger and more emotionally intelligent. We are adaptable beings; this is the foundation of our evolution. Similarly, as we adapt to new environments and circumstances, we can adapt our emotions to events.

## The Jungle Illustration

Let's imagine that you have a reason to live in the jungle. You encounter a tiger, and you are overtaken by fear as you worry about how to survive being eaten up by the hungry beast. You begin to run, hoping to save your life. The tiger sees you and begins to chase you. Luckily, you spot a branchless tree and climb to the top to escape. The tiger attempts to rise after you. After trying so many ways to climb the tree and none seem to work, it gives up and goes away. Your fear and worry lessen every second until the tiger is out of sight, and after a while, your fear disappears and you return to your normal emotional state.

Now, let's talk about what just happened.

You were in a near-death situation; in other words, a problem that triggered a series of emotions, but you eventually made it through. Since that was your first experience with such a life-threatening problem, it's fair to say that the emotions you felt were justified. If such a situation should recur months later, maybe with a lion, what would you do?

You have been faced with a similar challenge, but now, it's a different day and a different animal. Should you feel the same emotions you felt the first time, or should you immediately respond by finding that same tree that saved you the last time and climb it?

Giving in to worry and fear will not get you out of any problem, is it? No! If your emotions did not save you from the tiger in your first encounter, why should it save you this time from the lion?

Hopefully, this example helps you see that you do not have to go through the same emotional pain every time you are faced with a problem in your life. Instead of triggering emotions that cannot help you, build up your emotional strength. Of course, you are not expected to go completely numb to your emotions when life-threatening issues arise, but what matters is how you react.

There will always be a new problem or situation that will come your way, one that would want to trigger your emotions. However, for the most part, if you pay enough attention to your experiences, you will realise that you are usually faced with similar problems in your life, and somehow, you seem to always react the same way you did the first time.

For far too long, you have troubled yourself with trivial things; you get entangled in minor, personal problems and allow your emotions to blow them out of proportion, making them more significant than they are. Often, what you think are big problems are an exaggeration of the actual problem in your consciousness. As a result, you create worse suffering for yourself by adding layers of despair and misery to the actual situation.

## Regulate Your Inner Joy

You will always be faced with opportunities aimed at helping you evolve and mature emotionally. However, these opportunities may come to you disguised as challenges which you must deal with.

It's high time you stopped playing the victim when faced with challenges and started feeling good about the possibility of expanding your emotional capacity. My wish for you is that you realise that you can always feel good even amidst turbulence. No longer will you use any person or problem as an excuse not to feel good. You can always be joyful because your true nature is joyful and peaceful. You don't have to develop these or find techniques to be joyful; you were created with the innate ability to hold joy and peace. All you need to do is activate it.

When you were a baby, you were usually joyful, and nothing could make you worry or stress. You were mainly playful, happy, peaceful and free, regardless of what was happening in your awareness. But the moment you were mature enough to conceive thoughts, you began to worry and stress yourself over life's problems. Your joy went from being self-made to being dependent on people, circumstances, and your perception of the world. You deviated from your true nature and forgot that your default state is joy and happiness. But it's time for you to return home to your true self and nature. It's time to reunite with your true self.

## Consequence of Your Desires

You often have desires that cause you to live in sorrow or misery that make you forget about the present. In your mind, you project towards the future, focusing on the destination you desire rather than the journey you are embarking on. Imagine that you book a summer holiday month in advance to go to an exotic destination. The day before the trip, you pack your luggage and make some last-minute preparations. Then, on the day of your departure, you say to yourself, 'My starting point is home, and my destination is home. And since I am already home, I guess I don't have to go on this holiday.'

Wouldn't that be absurd?

Of course, it would be because you don't go on a holiday just for the end destination. You go for the fun and the experience. You go for the journey.

You mostly lack the patience to see your desire come to fruition. You almost want to drive everything with your desire's speed, which causes more tension and emotional resistance within you. You monitor and take the score on every move you make towards achieving your desires, and when you don't see the immediate results you wish, it steals your joy for another moment or for as long as you give yourself to it. This kind of lifestyle can be compared to a farmer who goes to plant seeds in his field. He weeds the farm, tills the ground, plants the seeds and waters them, then stands back expecting them to grow immediately. But when it does not happen that way because that is not the order of nature, he begins to panic, thinking about why his seeds have not grown according to his timing.

Sometimes, this is exactly how you treat your desires and end up stressing yourself out, worrying about things that do not matter. When your plans do not work out as you envisaged, you allow yourself to be weighed down by ill feelings, and that disappointment brings out more negative emotions from you, making you feel worse. A farmer should trust the germination process and understand that as long as he keeps watering the seeds and allowing some sunlight, they will grow with time. There is a gestation period for your desires, too, so you should stay joyful while being patient for things to take their natural course. Patience is not just the ability to wait but also your attitude in the waiting period.

## Your Desire Can Steal Your Joy

When you have a strong desire for something, what usually happens is that it begins to occupy your mind and becomes your most prevailing thought. Consequently, the desire, if not checked, will begin to cause you restlessness and unhappiness. For example, if you desire a car, you will believe that you will be happy when you finally get it. So, when you finally get it, you feel happy. But if we look at it from another point of view, you can ask yourself, 'Is there joy in the car itself?'

The answer is 'No!'

There is no happiness in the car. It was the meaning you assigned to the car that gave it so much power. When you wanted a car, you were restless, and when you eventually got it, the restlessness stopped; hence, you think it was the car that brought you joy. But it was the relief of the misery that brought back your joy. Remember that your true nature is already joyful, but unfortunately, you always put a condition on your joy. You have ignorantly conditioned yourself to think that you have to do or get something significant to feel this joy. It is this type of thinking that steals your joy.

Everything that you want, from the small desires to the big ones, are geared towards one thing: to make you feel good. The only reason you want them is because you think you will feel good when you get them. So, the primary reason is to *feel* good. But do you know that you can feel good right now wherever you are on your journey?

The problem with waiting to get the desire before feeling good is that you will always have a desire—man is a bundle of wants—and you will never stop desiring and wanting. Your daily experiences will always give birth to desires, no matter how big or small. This is human nature: you can never arrive at a state of complete satisfaction in all areas of your life; your list of wants will continually expand. There will always be something to reach for. From this base of understanding, if you are always waiting to get the next desire before feeling good, you can never enjoy your life journey. You have to make up your mind to feel good unconditionally and be intentional about being joyful if you must make the best of your life.

So many things can kill your joy and happiness if you give them power. When your desires are not met and you see someone else celebrating a desire that just came true, do you feel troubled? Your trouble is not only because you lack patience or you think life is not fair to you; it is also because you have been conditioned to believe that there is a shortage of abundance in this world and you are suffering from insufficiency. You think there is a pie of abundance, and every time someone gets a slice of that pie, there's less for you. This false programming triggers worry and unhappiness and causes your emotional pain.

The truth is, there is no shortage anywhere in the world. One way to convince you of this is to bring your mind to the little things like the air you breathe. You don't think about breathing when you wake up because you know there is enough air to go around—even if someone is gasping, it does not mean that you have to worry about your supply. This is the same way you should see abundance and desires. Never worry about a shortage of supply.

Desires are great, but if they cause you pain or constantly put you in a state of misery, you are going about it the wrong way. Find the middle ground between appreciating what is, while looking forward to what's coming. This is the sweet spot in living a joyful life: feeling grateful and satisfied with where you are right now even though you are eager for more.

## Feel Good

Feeling good should be your primary desire, and you are going to have to be intentional about it until you have successfully trained yourself to become natural with it.

I have outlined five ways that can help you stay joyful daily. These are not hard steps, and by doing them, you will experience the paradigm shift you need to become someone who always feels good regardless of the surrounding circumstances.

I.    Desire to feel good
II.   Think of ways to feel good
III.  Look for new ways to feel good
IV.   Do things that will make you feel good
V.    Encourage others to feel good


### i.    Desire to feel good

This is the foundation for the other four steps. If you don't desire to feel good, then you are never going to feel good. Desire is the basis for all achievements, and people who work hard to achieve their desires always reap the fruits. Unfortunately, the default state for most is to feel bad and beat yourself up. To build the desire to feel good, the first thing you have to do is develop a strong 'why' for it. Why is it essential for you to feel good?

Well, for a start, feeling good impacts your health, mental stability, and overall well-being. Without identifying your 'why' for feeling good and holding on to it all the time, it becomes easy not to. This desire sets the stage for the other steps to flow with ease.

## ii.    Think of ways to feel good

Once the desire to feel good is in place, you will have the capacity to unlock the thoughts and ideas you can use to feel good. So, as you plan for the day or week and see what you will do, where you will go or who you will meet, you keep asking yourself, 'What can I slot into my schedule that will make me feel good?'

Maybe it's to wear your favourite outfit or speak to a family member, to prepare your favourite meal or exercise. Whatever it is, you know how it makes you feel. Be intentional about planning for things that bring you pleasure, joy and peace, even though they are external things for now. Eventually, you will rewire your thoughts and emotions to always feel good.

## iii.    Look for ways to feel good

Most people spend their lives looking for occasions to be offended and hoping to find fault. The problem is that there is no shortage of reasons to be offended. If you keep track of everything that happens around you, you will find many faults throughout the day. So, not only is it vital to think of ways to feel good, but you should constantly be on the lookout for new ways to improve on the way you feel. Losing yourself in the service of others is one sure-fire way to feel good. Volunteer your time to help someone. The opportunities to feel good are always there, and if you become conscious of them, you will see them.

Have you ever bought a new car and immediately you start seeing the same model of the car everywhere? This is because, by owning the car, you are more conscious of that exact car, and so when you see someone else driving the same car, you notice it. The interesting thing is people have always been driving that car, but you did not take notice because you were not conscious of it. Similarly, the opportunities to feel good are always there, if you become conscious of it, you will see them, because what you seek is what you find.

So, as you have that meeting or talk to that person, be more conscious and always keep an eye out for these opportunities. When you are conscious in this way, they will be more obvious to you. They have always been there, but you were not "tuned" into them.

## iv.  Do things that will make you feel good

It is one thing to look for ways to feel good, and another to take the necessary action to feel good. To ascertain your level of consciousness in achieving this, take a 10-minute inventory of your day and ask yourself, 'What did I do today to feel good?' and 'What can I do tomorrow to feel good?'

Imagine if everyone took the responsibility to reflect on what they are constantly doing to uplift themselves in this way. This would put the responsibility back where it belongs: with the individual.

## v.  Encourage others to feel good

Doing things to feel good is great but encouraging others to feel good is even more powerful. How often do you encourage others to feel good? Most people spend their lives expecting others to make them feel good because they have programmed their joy to be people dependent. They are so dependent on people that if their request is not met, they see the other person as selfish, when in truth; it's actually selfish of them to have such expectation on others.

Encouraging others to feel good helps you to move from addition to multiplication of your joy. By encouraging others to feel good, you create a ripple effect around you because you share the good feeling with everyone you meet, thus increasing the overall joyfulness in the world. And by uplifting others, you feel good, too. You see, when you are feeling the joy of just yourself, you have one person to be happy for, but when you are feeling the joy of your team, acquaintances or your community, you've now got a million reasons to be joyful. There is a sense of fulfilment in lifting and helping others to feel good. Don't deprive yourself of this feeling.

The five steps discussed above are for every day, not some days, not once a week or once a year. From the moment you wake up in the morning till you go to bed, you should intentionally focus your mind on these feeling good patterns. As you apply these five methods to your daily life, you will begin to rewire your mind and develop the habit to always be on the lookout for ways to feel good.

As your effort towards feeling good becomes a daily routine, and then weekly and monthly, you are setting yourself up for incredible years ahead. When you feel good and encourage others to do the same, not only does your world change positively, but everyone and everything around you also benefit. In turn, you become a beacon of light and hope for others and more importantly, you know what it's like to operate in your true nature.

# CHAPTER 8

## CONTEMPLATING EMOTIONAL ADDICTIONS & TRIGGERS

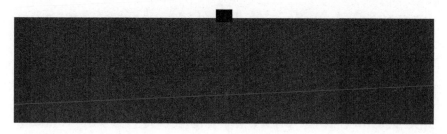

I f you don't learn to master and process your emotions, you will always find ways and techniques to avoid them. These techniques will almost always manifest in the form of an addiction in your life. In other words, without humility to your emotions, these addictions are inevitable. This has never been truer in my life as it is right now.

## A Taste of My Addiction

It was about 10am on a Thursday morning and I had just realised that I had a meeting at 1pm in the afternoon that I was ill-prepared for. I was tasked to give a presentation and showcase my work. Because the deadline was approaching quickly and I had nothing to show, a feeling of anxiety kicked in. I began panicking, and even though I wasn't hungry, I went to the kitchen and grabbed a biscuit. I already had a big breakfast that morning at about 8am but I needed to chew on something. I returned to my desk and started putting some slides together. After struggling to put the first slide together, about 15 mins later, I stood up, went to the kitchen again and grabbed some chocolate and returned to my desk.

At about 11am, I still had not done much, even though I had been working on it for about an hour or so. Again, I went back to the kitchen to make some tea and toast and returned to my desk to continue working on the presentation. I wasn't really hungry but I needed to keep my taste buds active and busy. When I got stuck again, I stood up, went to the kitchen, opened the fridge and as I was about to grab a yoghurt, it hit me!

I paused and thought to myself, "You know what? I actually don't need this yoghurt. In fact, I am quite full, so why do I need to have this right now?" This was a defining moment for me. It was then I had my first conscious awareness of using food as a gateway to avoid feeling or processing my emotions. It made me wonder what else I do or don't do influenced by an emotion I do not want to feel. What were my emotional triggers?

## Deep Dive Into Addictions

Do you have any addictions? At first thought you may think you don't, and this is because you often attribute addictions to people who take excessive drugs, alcohol or people who consume too much food, TV, porn or people who over-exercise, play video games, or do any activities excessively that they don't have control over. In fact, for the most part, you only think of 'major' physical addictions when discussing the subject of addictions; hence you think you are completely free from addictions when, in fact, physical addictions are simply the expression of emotional addictions.

In order to understand emotional addictions, we need to look at how your addictions are created in the first place. Simply put, addictions are created when you have a will-based desire to not feel an emotion. In other words, when you have a desire to deny, suppress or resist the feeling of a particular emotion, then you are on your way to an emotional addiction, which will eventually become a physical addiction if it is not processed or challenged.

From a very tender age, you develop many addictions in various subjects of your life. These addictions are influenced by your family, friends, acquaintances, trauma and your environment in general. So, you become used to them and thus develop expectations.

As an example, let's say you were raised in a household where dinner was always made by your mother. Unconsciously, you may develop an expectation on who should make dinner or cook in the household. If you are a man, you may begin to expect your wife to do the cooking always. If this addiction is not challenged, when you have your own family, you would expect your wife to always prepare the meals. In this example, you can see that you don't have a physical addiction about the subjects, but there is an emotional addiction or expectation there.

If you came home one day after work, and your spouse did not prepare dinner, this in turn might trigger an emotion within you. And if you don't process or challenge this emotion, eventually you might turn to physical addictions to help you deal with the situation. You may yell at your spouse, and if they still refuse to cook, then you may develop a habit of using alcohol, drugs or something else to suppress the emotion.

## Cycle of Addictions

Do you know what addictions actually feel like? Have you ever wanted to do something so desperately that you get this overwhelming feeling to do it at that exact moment, and nothing else matters in that instant? Anytime you have a feeling of compulsion in this type of way, then you are more or less addicted to that thing. And when you feel the urge to do it, there are usually two things that can happen—either the addiction is satisfied or not satisfied.

When your addiction is satisfied, you feel fabulous and relieved because the expectation you have on that subject was met.

For example, let's say as a woman, you have an expectation that the man is responsible for taking out the garbage in the household, and you eventually end up with a man who takes the garbage out all the time. You will feel satisfied and 'happy' because your expectation was met. In addition, if you are a man and you have expectations that the woman is responsible for cooking dinner in the household, and you end up with a woman who cooks dinner all the time, then you will feel justified about your expectations and addiction. You will think your expectation is actually right!

As another example, if you are addicted to likes and comments on your social media posts, then whenever this addiction is met and you receive multiple likes and comments, you get a dopamine rush and it equally makes you feel good.

Basically, when your addictions are met, you feel 'loved'. This is important to recognise because you most often associate feeling loved with events or relationships where your addictions are getting met. But is this a feeling of real love or is it a facade?

When your addictions on various subjects in your life are being met in this way, you often seek more because you want to feel good, satisfied, justified and loved all the time. So, you demand for more of the addiction and as long as it keeps being met, you keep feeling 'loved' and this becomes an endless cycle of addiction until the addictions are eventually challenged.

Most people live their lives in this type of facade, which leads them further away from truth and further away from the desire to process their emotions and as a result they reinforce a lot of false beliefs about themselves and many subjects.

Conversely, when your addiction is not satisfied, you feel frustration, anger and sometimes annoyance.

Using the previous examples, if you are a woman and you have an expectation that the man is responsible for taking out the garbage in the household, and you eventually end up with a man who does not take the garbage out, this will annoy you. On the other hand, if you are a man and you have expectations that the woman is responsible for cooking dinner in the household, and you end up with a woman who refuses to cook dinner for you, you will feel dis-satisfied and angry. You may even yell at her or express your dis-satisfaction towards her. Similarly, if you don't get the likes and comments that you expected on your social media posts, you get frustrated and most times you feel unloved.

In contrast to when your addictions are met, when they are not met, you feel 'unloved'. This is also important to recognise because you most often associate feeling unloved with events or relationships where your addictions are not getting met. But again, is this feeling true or is it a facade?

When your addictions on various subjects in your life are not being met in this way, you don't like the negative emotion and you don't want to feel or process it and so you often get creative and look for other ways to meet your addiction so you can feel good again. You basically look for the feeling of love in other places. In the case of your wife not cooking for you (if you are the man), you may result in stopping by a nice fast food restaurant to grab a meal before coming home. This behaviour can become addictive. The addiction cycle also applies here because you will keep looking for the feeling of 'love' in other places and in other ways as long as your addictions are not being met. As a result, you create a multitude of addictions in your life that range from small to medium to large.

On any given day, you may have up to fifty addictions that you employ before lunch time and you are not even aware that they are addictions.

The goal is to try to see when and where these addictions are at play in your life and begin to challenge them. When you do, you will start questioning some of your choices.

Like me, you may find out that you have a compulsion to eat something when your addiction is not being met or you don't want to feel a certain emotion.

These addictions are more in display in relationships. Most single people have created a whole lifestyle that supports their addictions so they never get challenged, and if they do, they just withdraw quickly from that relationship. And when they do, they feel relieved, safe and in 'control' again.

They basically run away from the opportunity to *process* their emotions.

Another addiction most people have is the addiction to be heard. They want others to acknowledge their feelings. They want their suffering to be understood, their anxiety's noticed or they expect their feelings to be validated. When they get interrupted during a conversation, they get annoyed or irritated.

When they are furious or sad, they expect others to approve and justify their reasons for being furious or sad. And when these expectations are not satisfied, they get emotionally triggered and in most cases, it manifests in their actions, leading to physical addiction.

How do you know your emotional addictions are not met? Well, for the most part you will feel anger, rage or irritation.

## Physical Addictions

Think of every physical addiction as a manifestation of an emotional addiction that was not satisfied. Unfortunately, most people are getting their emotional addictions satisfied and for this reason they have a less likelihood to develop a physical addiction. The people with physical addictions are just demonstrating that their emotional addictions have not been met. So by the time the physical addiction is already in place, it indicates that there has been an emotional addiction that you have not dealt with yet.

When your emotional addictions are met, you won't go to a physical addiction to de-tune from the emotion. You only go to a physical addiction generally when your emotional addiction is not fulfilled, and you don't know how to meet it. The physical addiction can be drugs, alcohol, medications, pills, pain killers, TV, video, movies, porn, masturbation, regular partying, or even self-harm. These become your gateway to suppress your emotions.

You often look at people with physical addictions and shame them. If you are walking down the street in the middle of the day and you see some persons soaked in alcohol, you will probably judge them automatically. But in reality, the people with physical addictions are actually 'better off' because their addictions are visible and obvious. But the problem with majority of us is that, we hardly know we have an addiction problem because our addictions are being met all the time.

It's more difficult for the person who keeps getting

their emotional addictions met to realise their addictions, than for someone whose emotional addictions are not met. Just because you have not yet developed a physical addiction does not necessarily mean that you are in a better spot. It just means that you have become very skilled at suppressing your emotion. And a consistent suppression of emotions can manifest in a form of physical illness.

Generally, we are essentially living in an emotionally dark age. This means that for the most part, society has made the expression of certain emotions a bad thing. During the process of socialisation, children are punished for having certain emotions. When a child is crying, you see the parent try to tell them to stop. As a result, they disassociate from, reject and deny those emotions. They then grow up to suppress these emotions and deny they even have them. In school, children are punished if they express certain emotions. You see this happen in professional environments, where people are not allowed to freely express their true emotions. You also see this clearly in organised sports on television, where the players are no longer allowed to express their frustrations in the game without being penalised for it. So, without consciously knowing it, society has trained us to suppress our emotions.

## Challenging Your Addictions

I have outlined four steps that can help you challenge your emotional addictions daily. These are not hard steps, and by doing them, you will experience the paradigm shift you need to become someone who always feels good regardless of the surrounding circumstances.

I.   Acknowledge & Accept The Addiction
II.  Feel The Emotion
III. Don't Judge The Addiction
IV.  Don't Feed The Addiction

## I.   Acknowledge & Accept The Addiction

The process of deconstructing your addictions and reversing these behaviours begins when you become intellectually aware and acknowledge your cycle of emotional addictions. Once you are aware, you will become turned off to the fact that you are doing them and slowly, like a flower germinates over time, you will begin reversing your compulsions and addictions.

This step is not as easy as it seems. Before you can acknowledge an addiction, you need to be able to notice it; and in order to notice the addiction, you have to pay attention to your emotional patterns. How would you know you are in your addiction? Your emotions are your guide. When you mostly feel anger or rage or irritation or any form of dissatisfaction, this is your compass letting you know you are probably living an emotional addiction. And in that moment you can choose to feel the emotion.

Take notice when you feel the compulsion to do something. Notice what's going on in and around you or when you feel the urge to do something, make a move or take an action.

Examine your daily life and routines and all the interactions that are happening. You will start to recognise your subtle addictions.

## II.    Feel The Emotion

Intellectual awareness of your emotional addiction is not enough. You will have to become sensitive to the emotion and allow yourself to *feel* it.

As discussed in previous chapters, we can build emotional strength so we are not triggered by every external event we come across. However, if the triggers occur and we find ourselves consumed by certain emotions, we want to feel it. We are designed to feel every emotion. Not run away from it.

When you feel the emotional trigger, try to identify where the emotion is within your body. Do you feel in your stomach area? Is it moving fast or slow? Is it painful? Does it affect your breathing? Notice the texture of it and how it feels and allow it to pass through your body. You can put a timer and say to yourself, "For the next minute, I am going to feel this emotion on purpose". The emotion is just a vibration going through your body, and that's all it is really. It can't kill you. You can survive all of them. Life is 50% positive emotions and 50% negative emotions.

When you feel the emotion, you are taking responsibility and you are allowing the emotion to pass through and within you. You allow it to take its natural course of motion. By allowing the emotion to express itself in this way, you are releasing it. When you release the emotion, you will be able to connect to the causes of the emotional addiction.

The continuous act of doing this will enable you to become more sensitive to your emotions.

## III.   Do Not Judge The Addiction

It is important not to judge the addiction or judge yourself, as that in itself is an addiction. Don't get caught up in the shame or frustration of "I can't believe I am like this"

Judging the addiction causes us to ignore the addiction that you are trying to process in the first place.

## IV.   Do Not Feed The Addiction

If you feed the addiction then you end up in the cycle of emotional addiction. But if you stop satisfying the addiction, it will expose the emotion driving it. You want to expose the cause so you can reverse it. If you do not get to the root cause, you may never be able to give up the addiction.

So, the next time you develop the urge to engage in something like playing a video game or snacking in between meals, pause for a moment and examine how you feel. Ask yourself, "What thoughts occupied my mind just prior?" or "What event preceded the urge for this action?" You may realise that you are running away from an emotion.

With this realisation, simply sit with the emotion. Do not engage in the act. Just observe the emotions and feelings of the urge. Even if you decide to still engage in the act from this new awareness, it's still better than

~

not knowing. Notice your response to getting it met and recognise that feeling from a new perspective.

Doing this continuously will change how you look at the act, and in time you will no longer want to be driven by an emotional addiction and be able to reverse it.

I would like you to take a pause here and think about your emotional addictions. What are those things that trigger you emotionally? What actions or urges do you engage in after the trigger? Write them down and explore them individually. Using the steps outlined above try to process them one at a time, without any self-judgement. The aim is to savour the feeling but do not become the emotion. Witness it; allow it, and release it.

# CHAPTER 9

## FEEL WORTHY WITHOUT JUSTIFICATION

If you were asked, 'Do you digest your food?' your first response will probably be, 'Of course, I do. Every time I eat, I digest my food'. After all, who doesn't digest their food, right? Although this is undoubtedly true, I am inviting you to re-read the question and consider what causes your digestive system to function the way it does.

The moment you put some food in your mouth and start chewing, your digestive system wakes up like a motor engine with pistons and gears, and as you swallow your food, it picks up the food pieces, grinds and breaks them down further. It somehow knows how to separate the nutrients from the waste and where to send them throughout your body. This happens without your consciousness because that is the way these organs in your body have been programmed. They do not need your assistance to carry out their functions. Does this not make you feel grateful?

Right now, your heart is pumping and blood is running through your arteries and veins; in fact, it has been doing so since you were in your mother's womb. It pumps blood steadily even while you are sleeping. You don't consciously have to think or worry about this.

You breathe in and out every second without thinking about it. This happens almost on autopilot so that you can stay alive. You have the ability to think and reason. You have been blessed with the faculty of imagination to allow you experience anything and everything you want in the present moment. Wherever you are, thoughts and ideas flow to you constantly as if there are universal forces directly focused on you. You have emotions that act as signals, letting you know how you feel about a particular experience, event, place or thing.

Your eyes are perfectly calibrated to translate vibrations into sight. Your ears are designed to translate vibrations into sound; your nose and tongue let you identify smell and taste, respectively. You use these faculties non-stop each day without actively thinking about it.

When you cut or bruise yourself, your body heals after a few days or weeks, depending on the severity of the injury. This means that there is a power that is always available to look after you. This same power is responsible for growing your hair and nails even when you cut them. The cells and organs in your body cooperate in alignment to keep your body running successfully. In fact, you are a highly complex, self-sustaining, intelligent, dynamic, technological-advanced biological system. Does this not make you feel like a big deal?

Imagine what would happen if complete control of your bodily functions were assigned to you for just an hour. What do you think would happen to you? You would have to consciously focus on your heart to make sure it continues to pump blood. At the same time, you would have to make sure the physical translations of sight, sound, and other senses are working every second so you can experience your world effectively. You would have to be conscious of all your cells and organs to ensure they all work in harmony. And whenever you eat, you would have to deliberately digest your food and accurately oversee the separation of nutrients from waste, ensuring that each one goes through the appropriate channel and undergoes the fitting process as necessary for your body. Do you think you can efficiently handle these roles without crashing?

If someone started a conversation with you at this time, you would have to be able to think and reason and still control all these functions. Are you starting to get the essence of this conversation? In truth, you will not be able to handle all the complexities of your bodily systems for 5 seconds before you forget to breathe!

Does this not make you appreciate what and who you are?

The planet you live in is constantly rotating in perfect proximity to the sun. The sun comes up to warm up the planet and goes down each day, the moon lights up the planet when the sun is down, the wind blows, the clouds are moving, the rivers flow, the rain falls and the flowers are growing. Life is constantly *dancing* without your focused effort nor control. There is a power that keeps everything steady and flowing. It governs everything for you. The same power takes care of you on an unseen level without your request or acknowledgement.

You are its focal point.

In fact, doesn't it seem as though everything about

the laws of nature and the universe is designed to look after you so you can enjoy your experience here on earth? Does this not make you feel loved?

Do you not feel worthy?

The next time you look at yourself in the mirror, ponder on this idea.

## The Struggle to Fit In

If you struggle with feelings of unworthiness, you are certainly not alone. The life that you have lived has probably been the reason for this struggle. For me, this started at a very young age. Being the youngest and the only boy in my family, I was overly protected and discouraged from having too many friends. All I had for company were my three older sisters, whom I found difficult to relate with at times as we did not share the same interests. Also, they were more confident than I was and so I spent a lot of time by myself, in my head. As a result, I quickly became an introvert. With few boys my age to relate with and being protected the way I was, I started comparing myself to my sisters. This led to me thinking I was inadequate.

When I was seven years old, my parents put me in

a costly private boarding school even though they could barely afford the bills. I found myself amongst rich kids with whom I could not fit in. I remember an occasion when I was unloading my provisions into my wardrobe in my dorm room, and everyone turned to look at me. Without a single word spoken, I knew they knew that I did not belong as I had only a few things to unpack, while they all resumed with an abundance of provisions. You can't imagine the shame mixed with unease and humiliation I felt that day. That moment set the scene for several years of unspoken judgement.

I also remember not being able to spend money during lunch breaks like the other kids.

When school resumed and my classmates shared stories on the countries they visited and the things they bought, I avoided those conversations as I had no exciting stories to share. My holidays were the typical experience of a person from an average home. This left me exclaiming things like, 'I am not good enough because I cannot do the things they do'. I started comparing myself to them, and as the years passed, my self-esteem was affected by constantly feeling and thinking this way. I always felt inferior and inadequate when it came to my schoolmates.

On the surface, everything seemed fine; in fact, I was mostly happy and playful, but I also had a deep sense that something was *wrong* with me. Throughout my junior high school, I was never the object of anyone's attention. I always felt like I did not belong there, like a square peg trying to force itself into a round hole. I subsequently developed a lack of confidence in myself.

I remember an incident during our school sporting activity where I was to take part in a 4x100m relay race. About 20 minutes before the race began, I pretended to be sick because I was intimidated by the other runners, even though I had been preparing for the race for weeks. That was how intense my lack of confidence and inferiority complex had become. It affected my grades and general ability to excel in anything.

At the age of 14, I relocated to the Netherlands with my family. I had to start a new school, adjust to new communities and new people. Of course, I had a culture shock. Being in an all-white school where my skin was different from everybody else did not help. This further worsened my sense of self-worth.

It felt like everyone could be themselves, but not me. I carried around this burden of setting the right example for everyone who shared my skin colour. I felt like I had to wear a mask to just get through the day. Doing this over and over for years sabotaged my sense of worth.

In my senior high school, I decided that the best way to cure this feeling of unworthiness was through perfection. I thought that if I were just perfect, I would fit in. I assumed that if I strived to be the best in all I did, I would be noticed for the right reasons, which would boost my chances of being accepted and loved. So, I embarked on the journey to perfection. I threw myself into basketball; I signed up for dance classes and other extracurricular activities.

Much later, I observed that my self-esteem was high when I performed well, and it crashed when I had a poor performance. Indeed, my expectations kept fluctuating as a result of my performance. In college, being busy became my way of attempting to feel worthy. I worked hard to get the best grades with the expectation that it would make me feel worthy. I went into relationships hoping to fill the void. I thought that if I could find someone to love me, I would feel worthy.

Unfortunately, none of these attempts yielded anything tangible. Neither the perfection nor the constant busyness nor the relationships helped me attain the high self-worth I envisaged. These brief achievements may have made me feel great for a moment, but the feeling would eventually slip away when things didn't work out, and I would return to the status quo.

Can you relate to my unworthiness journey? Do you share a similar experience?

Many other reasons can make a person feel unworthy. For one, advertisers tell you that you need to possess certain things to belong or be accepted. Your parents may have shown you more love only when you were good, thus sending you a subconscious message that your worth is based on your actions. Similarly, the educational system taught you that your value as a student is based on your grades. When you get a good grade, you are celebrated and when you don't get a good grade, you are not.

If you have gone through any form of trauma or abuse, this can make you feel inferior to others. If you consume social media content regularly, you may start to believe that your value is based on the number of followers you have or the likes you get.

Social media in general, has given great room for misinformation and misinterpretation of many things. Many use their social media platforms to project only what they want others to see, mainly the good side of their lives. This creates a wrong impression in the minds of their followers. On the other hand, it projects a mirage for those who get carried away by the half-truths or outright falsehood. It draws people into the sea of inferiority complex while many others go the extra mile to falsify their lifestyles to keep up. Such a quest is futile at the end of the day, and the realisation that your self-worth is not dependent on other people's perception of you becomes glaring.

What would you have the courage to do if you felt worthy without any justification? What would your life look like? And what would you stop doing? Wouldn't you like to know? Your life could be a lot simpler and peaceful if you begin to feel worthy without justification. The fact is, you are worthy and unique as you are! There is no one like you on the planet. You have a unique set of values, experiences, knowledge, gifts, and talents. Some of these you were born with; others, you acquired and nurtured in the course of life.

For this reason, you should never compare yourself with anyone. Comparing yourself to others would be like a five feet tall basketball player who plays the point guard position, comparing himself to his teammate who is seven feet tall and plays the centre position. Each person has a unique skill set, yet they play complementary roles on the court.

The fact that no one else shares the same fingerprints with you is proof enough that you are supposed to be distinct. No one can be you, and this is your superpower.

Embrace it and recognise that you are enough by just being you. Your days of relying on external stimulants for your sense of worth are over. Begin to appreciate yourself for who you are. Appreciate your insecurities, weirdness, quirky giggles, awkward laughs, crooked smile, and unusual way of thinking about things. It does not matter what you have gone through to arrive here. What is most important is where you go from here. All the experiences you have gone through shaped you to be the unique person you are now.

When I flashback to my ordeals while growing up, though they were not all pleasant, I have realised that I experienced them for a reason. I have also learned lessons from them, which is why I can now teach and explain to people from my own experience. As they say, 'Experience is the best teacher'. If I have not been a victim of an inferiority complex and lack of self-worth, I would not be able to enlighten you about it.

The bottom line is anyone who tells you that you are less than who you are is only giving you false information. You do not need to regret anything about your life, be it your physical appearance, experiences, or lack of achievements. The accumulation of all of these makes you the unique person that you are. Remember that you have to first accept yourself for who you are, which will, in turn, make you acceptable by others. In my case, being an only son, had I accepted everything about my existence, I believe I would have had fewer struggles to contend with. I was too young to understand this then, but now, I am older and wiser. I remain grateful for all my experiences, and I think you should be, too, because they make you who you are.

If you feel these words resonating with you, do not let go of them.

# CHAPTER 10

## LOOKING FOR LOVE IN ALL
## THE WRONG PLACES

Whenever you hear or see the word 'self-love',
what is the first thing that comes to mind?
What does it mean to you, and what picture
does it paint in your head? When you treat yourself to a
nice meal or go somewhere cosy by yourself to refresh,
do you perceive that as an act of self-love? When you go
for a massage or book a spa treatment to get a manicure
or pedicure, does this mean you express self-love? When
you put on your favourite outfit and make yourself look
good on your way to a dinner date, is this you loving

yourself? When you buy yourself a new car or purchase a new, serene home, do you feel you love yourself?

While all these could be seen as outward expressions of self-love, there is more to it. The true meaning of self-love transcends just the giving or receiving of gifts or treats. It goes beyond self-care.

## What Does Self-love Mean?

If you define love only through good treats, does it mean you do not love people if you do not give them special treats?

Hopefully, you understand that expressing your love for someone goes beyond the material things. You usually give them affection, attention and appreciate. However, this also applies to loving yourself. You must express it in words, too. Tell yourself how much you love yourself as many times as possible; those words of affirmation go a long way.

In the same way, self-care does not necessarily imply self-love; it is your responsibility to care for yourself. However, loving yourself profoundly and affectionately requires extra effort and intentionality. True self-love doesn't only come from the acquisition of material things for self-pleasure or the favour from external circumstances but first, from accepting and appreciating yourself as you *are*. It is being content with and embracing yourself the way you are, not who you were or who you are going to be, but who you are right now!

Self-love begins the moment you realise your value and decide to treat yourself with the respect you deserve. It is when you look at yourself in the mirror and say to your reflection, 'I love you because you are unique, and you are enough!' That is self-acceptance. It is the beginning of your journey to self-love. Self-love requires you to talk to yourself and keep in touch with your true self every day like you would with someone you love.

## Living in Self-love

Self-loving is a state of appreciating and caring for yourself as you are. This love for yourself motivates you to gradually and intentionally facilitate a series of actions that help you take proper care of your well-being. I used the word intentional here because it is something you do consciously. You have to realise that you are your priority and have to take yourself seriously. In all sincerity, no one can do this job better than you; you are in the best position to ensure that you stay well and happy at all times irrespective of the prevailing circumstances. When your happiness and well-being become your primary goal, it is achievable and sustainable in the long run.

The importance of self-love can never be overemphasised, especially since it has to do with your well-being. It motivates you to make healthy choices for yourself, including your physical, emotional, and mental wellness. They are essential aspects of your life, and a breakdown of any of them can cause a total breakdown of your entire being.

You may struggle to talk to yourself in a loving way or love yourself right because you know more about yourself than anyone else. You know your quirks, awkwardness, bad habits, flaws, secrets, fears, and everything that could be used to describe you as an unflattering person best!

With this deep knowledge about yourself, you gradually develop the habit of always seeing the worst in yourself. You start picking on everything you do. By so doing, you grow to become your own worst critic, punching yourself hard and magnifying your errors. Consequently, you kill your self-esteem and confidence and fill yourself with bad energy.

Each time you look at the mirror, you always find reasons to probe, condemn, criticise, and judge yourself. You are not satisfied with the shape of your nose, the size of your ears, or the length of your hair. You think your tummy is bulging out in an ugly way, or you wish you could change one thing or the other about yourself. You wish your head and jawline had different dimensions from what you have on your face; perhaps, you have figured out a facial shape that is best for the perfect person you wish you were.

You may also have gone through a series of trauma, grief, heartbreak, or any other form of adversity familiar to man, and thus, caught a string of shame and other insecurities that make you feel uncomfortable with being yourself.

The best way to handle shame is to reach out to somebody you trust and confide in them. Share your story and fears with them to get help and reassurance. We all need someone to talk to at one point or the other in our lives; it is in no way a sign of immaturity or weakness to seek help or counseling.

. I'm sure you do not want to be stuck in the captivity of these negative emotions or want them to keep weighing you down and holding you back from living your best life. If you can share them with someone you trust, someone who cares about you and has your best interests at heart, you will receive words that will soothe your heart. Calmness will return to your mind, and you will begin to love and appreciate yourself for who you are, thus, igniting genuine self-love.

Shame cannot survive exposure.

Another reason it could be hard to love yourself is if you are a perfectionist. Perfectionists always want to get it right all the time, at first try. They do not want even a trace of error in their lives or affairs. Sometimes, they put in more than is necessary to make sure that they get it right. However, when everything crumbles, or a minor error sneaks in, they become depressed, disappointed, and sometimes aggressive. They made room for everything except the probability of life and the reality of our human fallibility.

However, at the core of perfectionism lies fear and shame. If you are a perfectionist, all that will consume your thoughts will be avoiding criticism, blame, and ridicule. You will become so conscious of what people will think about you and the report they will give about you or your work that you neglect your happiness, emotions, and opinions. But this does not help you in any way; instead, it brings you to a place of frustration where you punish yourself for every little mistake you make.

Instead of seeing mistakes as a learning process to become better at what you do, you see them as a hindrance to your success and attaining perfection. However, your frustration will not stop you from making even more grievous mistakes in the future; as humans, we are far from being perfect, but therein lies the opportunity for continuous growth. So, instead of striving for perfection, strive for continuous improvement.

You often forgive others for what they did, but have you forgiven yourself? The process of forgiving yourself is not always a smooth journey. You find yourself rehashing the hurt and occasionally overwhelmed by a burning desire for vengeance when you think about past events that hurt you.

But lack of forgiveness creates stress. It hinders you from enjoying total freedom, from moving forward in life. Forgiveness is the best way to get complete healing from hurt and be free from any form of emotional hang-up. It brings all the suppressed emotions to the surface so you can release them.

Developing the self-discipline to confront your deep emotions, deal with them, forgive yourself, heal, and move forward in life is a brave act of self-love. It means you love yourself enough to sit with yourself and work towards overcoming hard wired-thoughts and emotions that are not serving you rightly.

## Building Self-Respect and Inner Peace

How do you build self-respect?

You do it by consistently doing what is right in every situation, not minding if someone is watching you or not. For instance, you feel like seeing a trending movie, but you decide to meditate instead because of the benefits, or you are tempted to eat unhealthy meals or junk foods, but you go to the gym instead. That discipline and consciousness of doing making the right choices that are better for you long term, helps you build self-respect. This self- respect will help you to fall in love with who and what you are becoming.

Making and keeping promises to yourself is another way you can grow in intimacy with yourself. The way you appreciate and respect people who make and keep promises to you is the same way you will appreciate and respect yourself. This will encourage you to do more.

Life's greatest betrayal is the inability or failure to love one's self first before attempting to love other people.

If you want to be thoughtful, or you want to live a peaceful life, it all starts with re-connecting and tuning in to your inner self. When you are aligned with your higher self, It will bring back your full mental power and put you in total control of your activities, life, and what's going on around and within you. You will become more present in every second and minute of your life; you will develop the strength to respond rather than react to the challenges that life throws at you. You will be able to control and monitor the thoughts that come up in your mind and decide whether you want to nip it in the bud or allow it to blossom and push you into action. You will become conscious of those unwanted thoughts and be able to catch them before they are immersed into your subconscious. For the most part, you will never let an unwanted thought slip through your awareness to dominate your mind or steer you from the right thought.

You will stop looking for love in all the wrong places, because you will eventually recognize that you are *love*.

# FINAL CHARGE

I t is not a coincidence that this book showed up in your experience at this time in your journey. It may seem as though you controlled the series of events that brought this book to your world, but something led you here. There is something your inner guidance would like you to take as a lesson from this book. For some, it could be a lot, and for you, it could be just one thing. Whatever it is, I hope you found it here.

One of the greatest things you can discover in your lifetime is yourself; because this sets up the foundation for everything else. It determines what type of experience you are going to have in your lifetime. You can either have a joyful experience or a miserable or depressing one. It all depends on your level of self-awareness.

My assurance to you is that as you take some of the ideas laid out in this book and apply them to your life, you will find yourself becoming more self-aware, gaining more self-confidence, improving your self-worth, self-image, and you will learn to love yourself more than you could ever imagine. You will also begin to reap the numerous benefits that come from genuinely loving yourself, which includes being peaceful.

However, it is also critical to understand that the transformation from who you have been to who you want to be will not be a walk in the park. Bear in mind that you may experience several feelings, such as doubt and discouragement. I want you to understand that it is normal to feel this way, so you don't have to give up and return to your old self just because of it. Don't be too hard on yourself either or begin to think that you have never gotten anything right. You can expect even more significant challenges as you embark on this journey.

Face the process, embrace the change and keep your purpose in mind. Look at the goal of becoming the new you as the great reward you must achieve, which will be more beneficial to you than giving in to the discouragement and challenges. Be motivated in knowing that right on the other side of your transformation lies the freedom you want and the self-love you need to live your life at its best.

Let this thought inspire you to keep pushing. As you keep at it, life will become more meaningful to you, and you'll be happy with yourself. You will find yourself doing more with less effort, and it will seem like time has slowed down for you to meet up with it. You will become more present with yourself, and life will become more fun. You will feel more purposeful, empowered, and led to move on with a sense of ease.

Best of all, you will find out that people are loving towards you because you are now operating at a higher and better frequency. The doorway to living a joyful life swings inward, not outward, and as you build that relationship with yourself, you peel off the dark layers that held you back and eventually, you will unveil your true nature.

Your journey beyond self-awareness never stops. But let this be ok, because the fun is always in the journey.

I would like to leave you with this quote:

*"The closer you come to knowing that you alone create the world of your experience, the more vital it becomes for you to discover just who is doing the creating"*

**- Eric Micha'el Leventhal**

*From Self With Love*

Frank Osayi

Printed in Great Britain
by Amazon

25726042R00079